THE (ALTERNATIVE) HISTORY
OF DRINKS

THE (ALTERNATIVE) HISTORY OF DRINKS

A UNIQUE TALE OF ALCOHOLIC CONCOCTIONS

DAN WILLCOCKS

MICHAEL ANDERLE

LMBPN Publishing
PMB 196, 2540 South Maryland Pkwy
Las Vegas, NV 89109

First US Edition, August 2020
ebook ISBN: 978-1-64971-089-5
Print ISBN: 978-1-64971-090-1

DISCLAIMER

Cocktails Through the Ages is meant as an accompaniment to fans of the *In Her Paranormal Majesty's Secret Service* fiction series. While the recipes and creations in this book are legitimate and can be replicated in real life, consumption of any beverages from the recipes in this book is at the reader's own risk.

The information in this book has been collated and researched to try to create the most historically accurate version of the cocktail. However, some information may be loosely transcribed to create a more wholesome experience in this book. Take this book with a pinch of salt since it is an accompaniment to a fictional universe.

Consumption of Alcohol:

LMBPN and its properties do not promote the consumption of alcohol by its readers. Please do not rely solely on information presented within this book. Always read labels, warnings, and directions provided on products before using or consuming the product.

You must be of legal drinking age to access the information within this book. Please familiarize yourself with the legal drinking age in your respective country and territory before attempting to recreate any of the drinks listed herein.

By purchasing this book, you acknowledge that there is a government warning concerning the health effects of consuming alcoholic beverages: Government warning: (1) According to the Surgeon General, women should not drink alcoholic beverages during pregnancy because of the risk of birth defects. (2) Consumption of alcoholic beverages impairs your ability to drive a car or operate machinery and may cause health problems. Drink responsibly.

UK Chief Medical Officers recommend adults do not regularly exceed: Men: 3-4 units daily, Women: 2-3 units daily. Drink responsibly www.drinkaware.co.uk

Allergens:

Please read the labels of all drinks and foods listed in this book for allergen advice.

Liability Waiver:

In consideration for you purchasing this book, you hereby release, waive, discharge and covenant not to sue the Company, subsidiaries, DBAs, affiliates, successors, contractors, agents, representatives and/or employees from any and all liability, claims, demands, actions and causes of action whatsoever arising out of or relating to any damage to your property or loss, damage or injury that you personally sustain, including death, whether caused by the negligence of the Company or its representatives or not while participating in Company programs, using Site content and/or attending Company Events in person, regardless of location. You hereby assume all risks to your property and your person, and in no way will the Company be liable to you for damages or injuries you sustain.

AN INTRODUCTION

For those who don't know me, my name is Genevieve King, and I've lived a rather long life. This book probably isn't the place to tell you all about that, but just know it's longer than the average Joe's. I've traveled the world and met big-name folks along the way, but I can identify every period in my life by one thing:

The cocktails I've drunk.

There's a special alchemy in the art of mixology. It's a science, and a worthwhile one at that—way up there with quantum physics and spectral fabric deconstruction, in my opinion. My good friend Hendrick might disagree, but he's old and stuck in his ways. There's an artistry in providing new flavors and fuels to satisfy everyone from the alcoholic to the connoisseur, and it's to this craft that I dedicate this book.

Cocktails have been a recurring theme in my life. Even as a little girl, I remember my father playing with various liquors and mixes and creating his own concoctions. Nothing ever made it farther than the experimentation phase, but the kitchen was always filled with the scent of his creations.

In the end, he settled on a favorite, the "Jack Rose," which you can find later in this book. He'd sit me on his knee as he drank, and whenever I smell that sour flavor, I get taken back to those memories.

Cocktails are time machines. They're triggers and teleportation machines as well, and something to help get you through the hard times. I've enjoyed cocktails in anger, in pleasure, in pain, in ecstasy, in sadness, and in triumph. The breadth and extent of options available out there is something to be marveled, and it's the reason they've held my attention for as long as they have.

They say that variety is the spice of life, and cocktails provide that for me. There's a drink for every occasion, and a drink for every individual (unless you're under twenty-one, in which case, you probably shouldn't be reading this book).

This book is a compilation of many of the best recipes I have had the good fortune to stumble across, sometimes literally. I've listed everything from forgotten treasures to popular essentials for the twenty-first century. I've provided a brief overview of where the drinks originated and tried to keep everything simple enough that even the most amateur mixologist produce good results.

Drinks are listed in order of their entry into the world, rather than their popularization—you won't believe the number of "posers" who believe the Mojito was created in this century—and this helps to tell some of the story of how cocktails have shaped the world we're living in today. History is a huge interest of mine (having lived through a lot of it), so we'll progress from the earliest mixes to the contemporary ones.

I don't claim to be a professional, I am nothing more than a student. Professionalism lies in my other skills (those of you who know my work will be familiar with what I can do), but I will always be an apprentice of the magic of mixology, and I thank you for taking the time to pick up this book.

It plays a small part in funding my ventures within the spectral world and the work that the King's Court and I continue to undertake.

Drink up friends, for country and glory,
Genevieve "Jennie" King
March 11, 2020

MOJITO (1500S?)
(CUBAN HIGHBALL)

Serves: 1

History

The Mojito has one of the longest and most convoluted pasts of all drinks and is one that excites, given the conflicting details of its creation.

A bearded stranger once told me as I was sitting in the smoke-filled tavern of the Lion and Snake in London that the Mojito's roots go as far back as the English pirate Sir Francis Drake.

Now, that is only speculation and hasn't been proven, but the story goes that the Mojito was invented as a cure for scurvy and dysentery. Aguardiente, mint leaves, lime, and sugar cane created a cocktail that boosted the immune system, and the added sugar kicked their energy levels into high gear.

Of course, another theory is that African slaves working in Cuban fields gave the Mojito its name, with "mojo" meaning "to cast a spell," and an alternative source claiming the drink was invented at the La Bodeguita Del Medio in Havana, where the bartenders raised a real splash with the promotional noise they made.

What to expect

The only truth that *I* know is that the Mojito is a solid little number. The mixture of rum, lime, and mint creates a refreshing concoction that should be a staple at any party and has been at many of mine.

Ingredients

- 2oz light rum
- 2 teaspoons sugar
- 6–8 fresh mint leaves
- Club soda
- 1 lime
- Mint sprig

Method

1. Throw sugar, mint leaves, and a dash of club soda into a glass (preferably a highball if you've got one available).
2. Mix well until sugar is dissolved and the flavor of the mint has been released.
3. Chop the lime in halves and squeeze the juice from both sides. If you're feeling fancy, drop one half into the glass.

4. Add the rum (*arrh*).
5. Stir.
6. Fill the glass with ice cubes.
7. Top with club soda.
8. Garnish with a mint sprig.

JACK ROSE (CIRCA 1698)

Serves: 1

History

I met a man once who could drink more cider than your average pig (pigs eat apples—get it?). Anyway, locals called him Applejack, but I just called him Steve, because that was his name. Why am I telling you this? Well, it's a fun anecdote, and it is somewhat related. Applejack is said to be America's first spirit, and records indicate that it was introduced in 1698 by William Laird, a Scottish immigrant who made his home in colonial New Jersey. Although the Jack Rose was popularized in the 1920s and '30s, Daddy was drinking this long before it became popular.

As with most drinks, it's a bitch fight to claim its creation. Two things are certain: (1) the Jack Rose came into being sometime between 1698 and 1881, and (2) Steve might have eaten a lot of apples, but he never drank Applejack.

What to expect

There's a little bit of sweet, there's a little bit of sour (they should rename this the "Rogue.") The dash of grenadine adds the rosy-cheeked kiss of the cherries, and honestly, this goes down real smooth in the summer.

Ingredients· 1.5oz Applejack brandy

- 0.75oz fresh lime or lemon juice (depending on your preference)
- 0.5oz grenadine
- Lime or lemon twist

Method

1. Add the brandy, lime or lemon, and the grenadine to a shaker, along with some crushed ice.
2. Shake until chilled.
3. Strain into your desired glass.
4. Garnish with your lemon or lime twist.

DARK AND STORMY (1806)

Serves: 1

History

RYAN GOSLING!

Now that I have your attention, this little snippet of history does contain a little Gosling. No, I don't know if Ryan is a direct descendent, and no, I don't mean baby geese...

In 1806, a sailor found himself in the midst of a storm on his way to Virginia. After weeks of fighting the elements, he didn't arrive in America, but instead made for the shores of Bermuda. With Gosling's history of spirits and liquors ingrained in his blood, he created the Dark and Stormy to commemorate his failed voyage.

Where some people see walls, others see obstacles to overcome.

What to expect

The Dark and Stormy is a pretty little number, and super

simple, too. Three ingredients make up this drink and, if I can give you one piece of advice, NEVER add lime juice, and DON'T swap ginger ale for the ginger beer. You'll be doing yourself (and Gosling) a disservice.

Ingredients

- 2oz dark rum
- 3oz ginger beer

Method

1. Fill a glass with ice cubes.
2. Add rum.
3. Pour in ginger beer.
4. Stir.
5. Did I really need to list these instructions?
6. Oh, garnish with lime wedge, if you want. I wouldn't, but hey...

SAZERAC (1838)

Serves: 1

History

Creole apothecary Antoine Peychaud invented the Sazerac back in 1838. The first iteration of this drink was served to his fellow masons in egg cups. The name of the drink apparently comes from Peychaud's preferred brandy, Sazerac-de-Forge et fils.

The dash of absinthe was added later for a kick of the "Green Fairy."

What to expect

A curious mixture of flavors, the Sazerac's signature taste will give you a sample of the old-timey mixed with the long-lasting maltiness of the whiskey. The absinthe adds a helpful dash of licorice for those who crave anise.

. . .

Ingredients

- 2.5oz rye whiskey
- 1 sugar cube
- 2 dashes Peychaud's bitters
- 1 dash Angostura bitters
- Absinthe
- 1 lemon peel to garnish

Method

1. Muddle a sugar cube with a few drops of water in an old-fashioned glass.
2. Add ice cubes, whiskey, bitters, and stir.
3. Dribble several drops of absinthe around the inside of a second glass until coated.
4. Pour out the excess.
5. Strain contents of first glass into second glass.
6. Garnish with lemon peel.

CANELAZO (1850)

Serves: 3

History

Like my great-grandfather, the origins of this drink are unknown.

Consumed mostly in the Andes, Ecuador, Columbia, and Peru, I came across the Canelazo while riding on the back of a mule and scouring the wastes for a poltergeist that had gone astray.

Little did I know that while I never did find that specter, I would stumble across a community who would keep me warm, fed, and watered. The Canelazo was one of the staples on their menu.

In modern days, the Canelazo is popular around Christmas and during Fiesta de Quito.

But that's for another time.

What to expect

Warm and spicy, the Canelazo is a great drink to calm down at the end of a long week or to forget that your relatives are getting under your skin while gathered around the dinner table caught in a game of Boggle or charades. Or so I've heard...

Ingredients

- 24oz water
- 4 cinnamon sticks
- 4oz sugar or grated panela
- Aguardiente

Method

1. Combine the water, cinnamon sticks, and sugar or grated panela in a medium-sized pot.
2. Bring to the boil, then reduce the heat.
3. Simmer for 30–40 minutes.
4. Mix in the aguardiente a bit at a time until the strength suits.

Bonus

If you like your Canelazo without alcohol, just forget the aguardiente and enjoy a hot spiced tea.

MANHATTAN (1860)

Serves: 1

History

Another one lost in the mists of time. Contrary to popular belief, I have it on good authority that a bartender named Black created this modern classic. First concocted on Broadway near Houston Street, the trend soon caught on, but has only been popularized in recent times by hipsters and fashionistas the world over.

What to expect

Bitter and sweet, the Manhattan can warm even the most frigid cockles on a Saturday night. Best enjoyed on an empty stomach to appreciate the finer flavors.

Ingredients

- Ice
- 3oz bourbon
- 1.5oz sweet vermouth
- 2 dashes Angostura bitters
- 1 Maraschino cherry to garnish

Method

1. Fill a glass with ice.
2. Add bourbon, vermouth, and bitters.
3. Stir and chill.
4. Strain into glass
5. Garnish with cherries.

WHISKEY SOUR (CIRCA 1870)

Serves: 1

History

First mentioned in a Wisconsin newspaper in 1870, the whiskey sour added a fresh twist to the already popular whiskeys of the world. Stories tell that the Whiskey Sour was officially created by a man named Elliott Stubb, and to him I say, good on you, boyo. You've helped me through some trying times.

What to expect

Egg. There's egg in this.

But don't let that throw you off! The egg only adds to the texture, providing a drink that goes down the throat silky smooth. You won't taste it. Unless you cook it. I suggest you don't do that.

Ingredients

- 1.5oz bourbon
- 1oz lemon juice
- 0.5oz sugar syrup
- 2 dashes Angostura bitters
- Half a fresh egg white
- Slice of orange and a cherry on a stick to garnish

Method

1. Combine bourbon, lemon juice, sugar syrup, bitters, and egg white.
2. Shake.
3. Strain onto ice-filled rocks glass.
4. Garnish.

GIMLET (1876)

Serves: 1

History

The Gimlet didn't become popular until the mid-90s. Before then, it was given to British Navy sailors to help them fight off scurvy. A method was found to preserve lime juice without alcohol, and some genius discovered that mixing with 114 proof gin with the lime created a hell of a party in his mouth. The rest, as they say, is history.

What to expect

A staple for gin-lovers, the Gimlet utilizes the sourness of the lime to give the gin a twist that kicks you in the mouth. Plus, if you're planning your next sailing trip, what better way to beat scurvy?

Ingredients

- 1.5oz lime juice
- 1.5oz gin
- Ice cubes
- Slice of lime to garnish

Method

1. Put your chosen glass in the fridge
2. Pour lime juice into a tall glass.
3. Add ice cubes and gin.
4. Stir until container grows cold.
5. Strain mixture into chilled glass.
6. Garnish with lime.

TOM COLLINS (1876)

Serves: 1

History

The first official record of this drink in printed works was in 1876, though its story can be traced back further than that.

A goofy joke with a short half-life, two years previous to its publication, a game was played among New York's patrons who would start conversations with the phrase, "Have you seen Tom Collins?" before proceeding to tell them that a man named Tom Collins had been talking ill of them at another bar. The end goal was to upset their friend enough to go looking for this fictional man.

Don't believe me? It's a real thing, check it out. Just search, "Tom Collins Hoax of 1874."

Man, I love pranks.

What to expect

Refreshing and invigorating, the Tom Collins is simple but should by no means be underestimated in its flavor and fizz.

Ingredients

- 1.5oz gin
- 0.75oz lemon juice
- 0.75oz sugar syrup
- 4oz chilled soda water
- 1 slice of lemon to garnish

Method

1. Combine ingredients.
2. Fill a Collins glass with ice.
3. Strain drink over ice.
4. Stir gently.
5. Garnish with slice of lemon.

GIN RICKEY (1880S)

Serves: 1

History

Originally utilizing the lung-burning powers of bourbon in Washington DC during its first iteration, the Gin Rickey didn't take off until George A Williamson and Colonel Joe Rickey mixed it up and switched in gin as the anchor with which to pin this drink.

What to expect

A classic highball, the Gin Rickey is refreshing and simple. It leaves a tickle on the tongue and warms the heart. What else do you need?

Ingredients

- 2oz gin

- 2 tablespoons lime juice
- 4oz club soda
- 1 lime wedge to garnish

Method

1. Fill a highball glass with ice.
2. Pour gin and lime juice over ice.
3. Top with club soda.
4. Garnish with lime wedge.

MARTINEZ (1887)

Serves: 1

History

Walk down the street and ask a stranger, and you'll soon discover that not many people know of the Martini's older brother, the Martinez.

First printed in 1887, Professor Jerry Thomas is credited with the creation of this sweet drink, which was purportedly concocted while working for a patron traveling to Martinez.

What to expect

The maltiness of the gin combined with the sweetness of the vermouth creates an explosion of flavor on the tongue. The Maraschino liqueur is just the cherry on top of the cake (see what I did there?)

Ingredients

- 1.5oz gin
- 1.5oz sweet vermouth
- 1 teaspoon Maraschino liqueur
- 2 dashes orange bitters
- 1 lemon twist to garnish

Method

1. Fill cocktail glass with ice.
2. Add gin, sweet vermouth, liqueur, and bitters.
3. Stir until cold.
4. Strain into glass.
5. Garnish with lemon twist.

MARTINI (1887)

Serves: 1

History

James Bond's classic drink, the Martini is a symbol of class and sophistication.

Unless you've seen my aunt pissed out of her brains on the stuff. You can't get vomit out of cashmere.

One report in history claims the Martini was invented in the town of Martinez, where it is known as the "Martinez Special." I don't know if that's true. We do know is that somewhere down the line, the name was changed to acknowledge the subtle distinguishing features between the Martini and its predecessor, the Martinez.

What to expect

Shaken or stirred (don't shake it), the martini has a smooth, dry flavor and accompanies any black-tie event perfectly.

.   .   .

Ingredients

- 2oz gin
- 1 tablespoon dry vermouth
- Olive or lemon peel to garnish
- Ice

Method

1. Combine gin, vermouth, and ice.
2. Strain into martini glass.
3. Garnish with olive or lemon peel.

OLD FASHIONED (CIRCA 1889)

Serves: 1

History

According to the books, the Old Fashioned was created by Martin Cuneo in Pendennis Club, Louisville. The drink was made for a Kentucky Colonel between 1889 and 1896 and has carried through the ages.

What to expect

The bitters add complexity to the bourbon, and the sugar brings out the sweetness. The Old-Fashioned leaves a satisfying aftertaste and it looks great in the glass of the same name.

Ingredients

- 1 sugar cube
- 2–3 dashes of Angostura bitters

- 2oz bourbon
- Ice cubes
- Orange or cocktail cherry to garnish

Method

1. Combine whiskey, bitters, and sugar cube in a mixing glass.
2. Add ice cubes.
3. Stir rapidly to chill.
4. Strain into rocks glass with fresh ice.
5. Garnish with orange or cherry.

MAMIE TAYLOR (1899)

Serves: 1

History

A famous opera singer Mamie Taylor maintains her legacy through the very drink she once requested a bartender to make in her honor. I've tried several times to have someone make a drink for me, but they all say they can't capture my uniqueness. I don't blame them. I am one of a kind.

What to expect

Not dissimilar to the Moscow Mule, the Mamie Taylor chooses whisky over vodka for its base, with the lime cutting through the sweetness of the ginger beer.

Ingredients

- 2oz Scotch whisky

- 1 tablespoon lime juice
- 6oz ginger beer
- 1 lime wedge to garnish

Method

1. Fill glass with ice.
2. Combine whisky and lime juice and pour.
3. Top with ginger beer.
4. Garnish with lime wedge.

SUMMER CUP (1900S)

Serves: 1

History

You'll probably be most familiar with this drink thanks to the power of advertising at public sporting events like Wimbledon. The Summer Cup is the raw breakdown of what was created by Mr. James Pimm.

With Pimms now a common drink across the world and best enjoyed in sunshine, you might think of skipping this one and going straight for the easy option. However, let me assure you that brewing your own doesn't just taste amazing, but it lets you feel like you can brew with the best of them.

What to expect

Fruity, sweet, a nice little kick in the back of your throat, the Summer Cup is best enjoyed while sunbathing in the tropics. Not so much in a London downpour. Believe me, I've tried.

. . .

Ingredients

- 1oz ginger liqueur
- 1oz gin
- 2oz cranberry juice
- 0.5oz lemon juice
- 0.5oz simple syrup
- Soda water
- Lemon twist to garnish

Method

1. Combine all ingredients except soda in a glass.
2. Add ice.
3. Stir until glass is chilled.
4. Strain into second glass.
5. Top with soda water.
6. Garnish with lemon twist.

AVIATION (1916)

Serves: 1

History

This purple drink is very, very purple. Created by Hugo Ensslin in the early twentieth century, the first published mention of this drink appeared in 1916. I'm not sure if the name refers to airplanes or pilots or anything else that may have been going on around 1916—let's not go there—but the Aviation has flown through time and still hits the metropolitan scene today.

What to expect

The Aviation is best known for its floral, citrus flavor. Sip this gin-based cocktail slowly and let the subtle tones carry you away on the wings of the angels.

Ingredients

- 2oz gin
- 0.5oz Maraschino liqueur
- 0.25 oz crème de violette
- 0.75oz lemon juice
- Ice
- Brandied cherry to garnish.

Method

1. Combine ingredients in shaker and mix.
2. Strain into glass.
3. Garnish with cherry.

GRASSHOPPER (1918)

Serves: 1

History
Grasshoppers are green. This drink is green.
History lesson over.

What to expect
The grasshopper is the cocktail equivalent of an after-dinner mint. Palate-cleansing and smooth, the crème de cacao adds a silky tone, and the crème de menthe leaves you feeling as though you've just downed mouthwash.
In a good way.

Ingredients

- 0.75oz crème de menthe
- 0.75oz white crème de cacao

- 0.25oz heavy cream
- Ice

Method

1. Combine crème de menthe, crème de cacao, cream, and ice.
2. Mix well.
3. Strain into chilled glass.

APEROL (PERFECT) SPRITZ (1919)

Serves: 10–12

History

The original recipe has supposedly remained untouched since its inception in 1919. Created in Padua by the Barbieri brothers, the Aperol Spritz became popular in the 1950s.

What to expect

Serving up to a dozen individuals, this spritz is great for a party. The lavender adds a floral twist on an otherwise sweet drink, and the lemon wedges add zing.

Ingredients

- 7oz red vermouth
- 7oz white vermouth
- 7oz gin

- 1 teaspoon dried lavender
- Soda water
- Ice
- Lemon wedges
- Lavender sprigs

Method

1. Combine both vermouths and gin into a bottle or jug.
2. Add dried lavender.
3. Stir and rest aside to infuse overnight (in fridge).
4. Strain 1.75oz per person into each glass over ice.
5. (Optional) Top with soda water
6. Garnish with lemon wedges and lavender sprigs.

NEGRONI (1919)

Serves: 1

History

The Negroni is a variation of the classic Americano. Like all great foods and drinks, the Negroni was invented in Florence, Italy, by Count Camillo Negroni (talk about narcissism).

What to expect

A refreshing beverage, somehow the Negroni manages a balance of bitter, dry, and sweet at the same time. It's deep, rich, wooden color has cemented its reputation as a summer drink, although they're great all year round.

Ingredients

- 1oz dry gin
- 1oz Campari

- 1oz red vermouth
- Ice
- Twist of orange peel to garnish

Method

1. Combine gin, Campari, vermouth, and crushed ice in a shaker.
2. Shake (duh!)
3. Strain into glass over ice.
4. Garnish with orange peel twist.

BLOODY MARY (1920S)

Serves: 2

History

Full disclosure, I didn't want to include this in this volume, but my publicist forced me to. I don't care all that much about Bloody Marys, but apparently it's a "classic" to be included in any cocktail book.

Claimed to have been invented by the bartender Fernand Petiot in 1921, there are a number of theories on where the Bloody Mary acquired its name: the Virgin Mary, the Caesar, the Michelada, and the Red Snapper, to name a few.

What to expect

Where to begin...?

There's vodka, tomato juice, Worcestershire sauce, hot sauce, garlic, herbs, and every other ingredient you'd need in your sauce. Some love it, others hate it; approach with caution if you've got a tongue that's maladjusted to heat.

. . .

Ingredients

- Ice
- 3.5ml vodka
- 17oz tomato juice
- 1 tablespoon lemon juice
- Worcester sauce
- Tabasco
- Celery salt
- Black pepper
- 2 lemon wedges to garnish
- 2 celery sticks to garnish

Method

1. Place a large handful of ice in a jug.
2. Add vodka, tomato juice, and lemon juice.
3. Add 3 shakes of Worcester sauce.
4. Add 3 shakes of Tabasco sauce (or more if you want to burn your tongue off).
5. Pinch of celery salt.
6. Pinch of pepper.
7. Stir until jug is chilled.
8. Strain into 2 tall glasses.
9. Top with ice.
10. Add celery stick and lemon slice to garnish.

HEMINGWAY DAIQUIRI (1921)

Serves: 1

History

Constantino Ribailagua brought this drink into existence in honor of his daiquiri-loving regular, Ernest Hemingway. I've personally never met either Constantino or Hemingway, but someone who creates something this classic and beautiful to celebrate one of the greatest writers of our time has my vote.

What to expect

Fruit, fruit, fruit. Mix the Maraschino with the grapefruit and the lime, and you've got yourself one hell of a fruity mix. It's almost as if the rum isn't there (though, it most certainly is). Add a touch of sugar for additional sweetness.

Ingredients

- 2oz white rum
- 0.25oz Maraschino liqueur
- 0.75oz grapefruit juice
- 0.5oz lime juice
- 0.25oz simple syrup
- Lime wedge to garnish

Method

1. Combine ingredients in a shaker except the lime wedge.
2. Fill with ice.
3. Shake.
4. Strain into chilled glass.
5. Garnish with lime wedge.

MIMOSA (1925)

Serves: 8

History

Popularized by the incomparable Alfred Hitchcock in the 1940s, the Mimosa began as a variant of the classic Buck's Fizz.

Four years after the Fizz's creation, Frank Meier invented the Mimosa as a kinder alternative to the Bloody Mary. Bonus tip: get a good quality sparkling wine for the best Mimosa.

What to expect

You'll be hard-pressed to find a true connoisseur at a brunch without the Mimosa. The orange juice can count as one of your five-a-day, and the sparkling wine adds the bubbly finish. Simple and elegant, sip and enjoy.

Ingredients

- 25oz bottle dry sparkling wine
- 25oz fresh, chilled orange juice
- (Optional) 4oz Grand Marnier

Method

1. Half-fill eight champagne flutes with wine.
2. Top with orange juice.
3. (Optional) Add 1 tablespoon of Grand Marnier per glass.

CLASSIC FRENCH 75 (1927)

Serves: 1

History

The evolved form of the popular nineteenth-century classic, the Champagne Cup, gin was added much later to create the Classic French 75.

A variation of this was first published in 1922, but the popular form you now see was introduced to the world in 1927 in all its glory. You might find recipes use cognac instead of gin, but if you want to stay true to form, then leave the gin.

The Classic French may be less well known by modern society, but this drink had at least *two* mentions in the legendary movie *Casablanca*.

What to expect

Looking for a simple drink that packs a punch? This cocktail is for you. Quench that thirst with citrus tones and the tingles of the champagne and enjoy the sweet sensation.

. . .

Ingredients

- 1.5oz gin
- 0.75oz fresh lemon juice
- 0.75oz simple syrup
- 2–3oz champagne
- Lemon peel to garnish

Method

1. Fill cocktail shaker with ice.
2. Combine gin, lemon juice, and simple syrup.
3. Shake.
4. Strain into champagne flutes until half-filled.
5. Top with champagne.
6. Lemon peel to garnish.

GIN SOUR (1929)

Serves: 1

History

Popular opinion suggests (because no one can ever settle on a true origin of a goddamn drink), that Harry MacElhone created this simple sour drink in London back in 1919. However, in his original recipe, he used crème de menthe. Later, in 1929, he swapped the crème for gin and made a drink that is worth writing about. You sure saved your ass in time, Harry.

What to expect

Liquor, lemon juice, and sugar. Prepare your cheeks to get dragged into your mouth as the sweet meets the sour and creates an explosion of flavor that will leave you wanting more.

Ingredients

- 2oz gin
- 1oz lemon juice
- Half-teaspoon superfine sugar
- Ice cubes
- 1 Maraschino cherry to garnish

Method

1. Half-fill shaker with ice cubes.
2. Combine gin, lemon juice, and sugar.
3. Shake until chilled.
4. Strain into sour glass.
5. Garnish with Maraschino cherry.

TEQUILA SUNRISE (CIRCA 1930S)

Serves: 1

History

Invented by Gene Sulit in the 1930s, the original variation starred tequila, crème de cassis, lime juice, and soda water. Originally served at the Arizona Biltmore Hotel, this drink didn't hit its popularity until the lime was swapped to orange juice and the grenadine dropped in to give the Sunrise its classic dusky colors.

What to expect

With the orange juice taking the edge off the tequila and the grenadine injecting additional sweetness, the Tequila Sunrise catches the eye and can be a great conversation starter at parties.

Ingredients

- 2oz tequila

- 4oz orange juice
- 0.5oz grenadine
- Ice cubes
- 1 orange slice to garnish
- 1 Maraschino cherry to garnish

Method

1. Fill highball glass with ice cubes.
2. Add tequila and orange juice.
3. Stir well.
4. Slow-pour grenadine around inside edge of glass.
5. Garnish with orange slice and Maraschino cherry.

CASINO (THE SAVOY) (1930)

Serves: 1

History

I wonder why I included this one...

As fans of mine will know, the Savoy Theater has a strong hold on my heart. The Casino (often referred to as The Savoy) is part of the "Daisy" family of cocktails and was first published in 1930 by Harry Craddock.

Essentially an Aviation with orange bitters instead of crème de violette, the Casino goes down smooth and keeps the legacy of my childhood alive.

What to expect

A floral taste, with a hint of cherries from the Maraschino liqueur, the Casino hits every note on the way down. Served well over ice, this is a smooth drink to end the day (and maybe enjoy a show with, if you're so inclined).

· · ·

Ingredients

- 1.5oz gin
- 0.5oz fresh lemon juice
- 0.5oz Maraschino liqueur
- 2 dashes orange bitters
- 1 Maraschino cherry to garnish

Method

1. Combine ingredients except cherry in shaker.
2. Shake.
3. Strain into glass.
4. Add Maraschino cherry to garnish.

MARGARITA (1938)

Serves: 1

History

The earliest telling of the creation of the margarita comes from the drink being created for the former Ziegfeld dancer Marjorie King—a woman allergic to most spirits, leaving only the option of tequila. The inventor, Carlos "Danny" Herrera concocted this baby at his restaurant way back in 1938.

What to expect

Sharp, tangy, zingy, and refreshing, the margarita sucks in those cheeks and leaves you wanting more.

Ingredients

- 1.5oz tequila
- 0.75oz triple sec liqueur

- 0.75oz lime juice
- Salt
- Ice cubes
- 1 lime wedge

Method

1. Chill glass.
2. Combine tequila, triple sec, and lime juice into shaker, fill with ice.
3. Shake to chill.
4. Run lime wedge around outside rim of glass.
5. Roll lime-slicked rim in salt to coat.
6. Strain into glass.

MOSCOW MULE (CIRCA 1941)

Serves: 1

History

The Moscow Mule was invented circa 1941, supposedly by John G. Martin and Jack Morgan. However, that's not the part of this story that's interesting.

Around the dawn of instant photography, Martin his hands on an early Polaroid Land Camera and got busy taking pictures of bartenders and their drinks. It was at this time that Martin's Company, the Heublein Drinks Company, acquired the brand-new Smirnoff Vodka. With a vodka in one hand and a copper Moscow Mule cup in the other, Martin showed the images to his other clients to show them what the competition was selling, stirring up a buzz and bringing the Moscow Mule to people's attention.

What to expect

Best drunk from a copper mug to add that extra chill factor, the Moscow Mule is great on summer days as well as for holidays, thanks to its strong ginger flavor.

Ingredients

- 2oz vodka
- 0.5oz fresh lime juice
- 4oz ginger beer
- 1 lime wedge to garnish

Method

1. Fill copper mug (or regular glass if unavailable) with ice.
2. Pour over vodka and lime juice.
3. Fill glass with ginger beer.
4. Stir well.
5. Garnish with lime wedge.

MAI TAI (1944)

Serves: 2

History

The showdown of the Mai Tai creation is fought between Donn Beach (1933) and Victor J Bergeron (1944). Donn appears to have been discredited by her long-time colleague, so the crown lies on Victor's head for this one.

What to expect

This tropical cocktail is considerably better than its namesake (Mai Tai is Tahitian for "good"). Put on your grass skirt and bathe in the sunshine, it's Mai TIME.

Ingredients

- 1.5oz white rum
- 0.5oz Cointreau liqueur

- 0.25oz lime juice
- 1.5oz pineapple juice
- 1.5oz orange juice
- 1 dash grenadine
- 1oz dark rum
- Ice cubes
- Lime wedge and mint to garnish

Method

1. Put ice and all ingredients minus garnish into shaker
2. Shake until chilled
3. Strain over ice.

WHITE RUSSIAN (1949)

Serves: 1

History

The White Russian was invented alongside the Black Russian in 1949 in honor of Perle Mesta, then the US Ambassador to Luxembourg. It's a simple alternative to the Black Russian, the only difference being the dollop of heavy cream.

Heavy cream makes everything better...

What to expect

White Russians are the adult equivalent of a milkshake. Thick, smooth, and goes down a treat on a hot day, the White Russian certainly takes a higher rank for me than its cousin, the Black Russian.

Ingredients

- 2oz vodka
- 1oz Kahlua
- 1 splash heavy cream

Method

1. Combine vodka and Kahlua in Old Fashioned glass with ice.
2. Top with heavy cream.
3. Stir.

PALOMA (1953)

Serves: 1

History

For some reason, cocktails used to make their debuts in pamphlets. Arghh...those annoying bits of paper that litter the doormat when you've been away for a few weeks.

Anyway...

The creation of the Paloma is attributed to Evan Harrison, although it was thought to have been invented by a rival tavern manager. We all love a bit of drama in the cocktail-sphere.

What to expect

Fans of tequila will love this. Tequila is the Paloma's foundation, though the grapefruit and sugar syrup take off a lot of tequila's famous bite. A perfect accompaniment for Mexican food, the Paloma is best served alongside enchiladas and at fajita parties.

. . .

Ingredients

- 2.25oz tequila
- Juice of half a ruby grapefruit
- 0.75oz sugar syrup
- 2.5oz club soda
- (Optional) Dash of lime juice

Method

1. Combine grapefruit, tequila, and sugar syrup.
2. Pour over tall glass of ice.
3. Top with club soda.
4. (Optional) Add a squirt of lime juice.

PIÑA COLADA (1954)

Serves: 1

History

Did you know that *Piña Colada* is Spanish for "strained pineapple?" Sounds less delicious, doesn't it? I found that out while sipping this cream-colored drink in the tropics. You can thank Ramón "Monchito" Marrero at the Caribe Hilton's Beachcomber Bar in San Juan, Puerto Rico, for this drink. Little did Ramón know how much he'd change the game with this fruity recipe.

What to expect

Close your eyes and think of the Bahamas. That's what you'll get from the Piña Colada. The coconut brings you visions of palm trees, the pineapple adds a summer zing, and the rum completes this little number.

. . .

Ingredients

- 2.5oz white rum
- 3oz pineapple juice
- 1oz coconut cream
- Ice
- 1 Maraschino cherry to garnish.

Method

1. Combine rum, pineapple juice, and coconut cream in shaker.
2. Fill with crushed ice.
3. Strain into glass.
4. Garnish with Maraschino cherry.

LONG ISLAND ICED TEA (1972)

Serves: 4

History

Bob Butt created the Long Island Iced Tea.

That's right. Robert "Rosebud" Butt invented the Long Island Iced Tea.

I'll let that hang for a moment...

Okay, so Robert Butt *claims* to have invented this popular East Coast fixture for an entry in a contest in which a new drink called for which featured triple sec. Who am I to argue? His name says it all...

What to expect

A dash of *every* white spirit (not paint stripper) and a dash of coke and lime create the Long Island Iced Tea. Impossibly, despite the amount of alcohol in this drink, the other ingredients do a great job of covering what should be overwhelming to a delicate palate.

. . .

Ingredients

- 1.5oz vodka
- 1.5oz dry gin
- 1.5oz tequila
- 1.5oz white rum
- 1.5oz triple sec
- 1.5oz lime juice
- Ice
- 15oz Coca-Cola
- 2 limes, cut into wedges

Method

1. Combine vodka, gin, tequila, rum, and triple sec in a large jug.
2. Add lime to taste.
3. Half-fill jug with ice.
4. Stir until chilled.
5. Add Coca-Cola to taste.
6. Add lime wedges.
7. Fill 4 glasses with ice cubes and pour iced tea over.

ESPRESSO MARTINI (1983)

Serves: 2

History

Originally christened the "Vodka Espresso" in 1983 by Dick Bradsell, the Espresso Martini is now a staple in the land of cocktails. For connoisseurs wanting an injection of the morning Joe in their alcohol, this one's for you.

What to expect

Bitter from the coffee yet sweetened by the Kahlua, the Espresso Martini gives you all the pleasure of your morning brew in an evening setting. Great for sipping, the Espresso Martini goes down smooth and gives you a sweet little boost of energy, too.

Ingredients

- 3.5oz vodka
- 1.75oz freshly brewed espresso coffee
- 1.75oz Kahlua
- 0.5oz sugar syrup
- Ice
- (Optional) 4 coffee beans to garnish

Method

1. Put 2 glasses in fridge to chill.
2. Pour 1 tablespoon of sugar syrup into shaker.
3. Add handful of ice.
4. Combine vodka, espresso, and Kahlua in shaker.
5. (Sigh…) Shake.
6. Strain into chilled glasses.
7. (Optional) Garnish with coffee beans.

COSMOPOLITAN (1987)

Serves: 1

History

The most popular theory of the Cosmo's creation is attributed to Toby Cecchini of Manhattan's Odeon in 1987, though this drink was truly made popular by the TV show *Sex and the City*.

What to expect

Fun, fruity, and ticking all the right boxes for a metropolitan night out, the Cosmopolitan your perfect companion for an easy night with your friends.

Ingredients

- 1.5oz orange vodka
- 0.5oz Cointreau liqueur
- 1oz cranberry juice

- 0.25oz fresh lime juice
- Ice cubes
- Orange zest to garnish

Method

1. Fill glass with ice to chill.
2. Combine all ingredients, except orange zest, in a shaker.
3. Shake.
4. Strain into glass.
5. Sprinkle orange zest to garnish.

THE FITZGERALD (CIRCA 1990)

Serves: 1

History

Born in the Rainbow Room in New York, the Fitzgerald played a fundamental role in the resurgence of the bar scene. Invented by Dale Degroff in the 1990s, he combined fresh ingredients to give the Fitzgerald its unique flavor.

What to expect

The freshness of the ingredients makes the Fitzgerald. Bottled sweetened sugars shouldn't touch this if you want an authentic experience. Fresh, and revitalizing, The Fitzgerald can really put a zing in your step.

Ingredients

- 0.75oz lemon juice

- 0.75oz sugar syrup
- 2 dashes Angostura bitters
- 1.5oz dry gin
- Crushed ice
- Lemon peel to garnish

Method

1. Combine ingredients in shaker.
2. Shake.
3. Strain into chilled glass.
4. Add lemon peel to garnish.

PENICILLIN (CIRCA 2000)

Serves: 5–6

History

The Milk & Honey bar chain was a pioneer in the cocktail game. First concocted in the early 2000s by Sam Ross, he paired sections of the Gold Rush with blended Scotch and sweetened the final mix with honey, syrup, and sweetened ginger juice.

What to expect

Scotch doesn't typically make a great base for creative cocktails. However, the Penicillin is well-balanced with its additional ingredients. With the honey-ginger syrup, there's a note of Christmas in this drink that can quickly fill you with festive cheer.

Ingredients

(*For honey-ginger syrup*)

- 4oz honey
- 4oz water
- 3-inch piece of ginger root

(*For cocktail*)

- 2oz blended Scotch
- 0.75oz lemon juice
- 0.75oz honey-ginger syrup
- Ice
- 0.25oz Islay Scotch
- Lemon peel to garnish

Method
(*For honey-ginger syrup*)

1. Peel and slice ginger root.
2. Combine honey, water, and ginger root in a pot and bring to boil.
3. Reduce heat and simmer for 5 minutes.
4. Let syrup cool.
5. Strain.
6. Store in fridge.

(*For cocktail*)

1. Combine Scotch, lemon juice, and syrup in a shaker.
2. Fill with ice.
3. Shake.

4. Strain over ice in glass.
5. Gently pour Islay Scotch over the back of a spoon to float.
6. Add lemon peel to garnish.

HEART OF DARKNESS (2000S)

Serves: 1

History

I'll be honest, the origins of this drink are as enigmatic as its appearance and flavor.

I would never have believed that charcoal could play an active part in a delicious cocktail, but the Heart of Darkness achieves that perfect balance of flavor and artful form. Garnish with a blue or purple orchid and place in a decorative glass, and you've found the most Instagrammable cocktail to have graced the twenty-first century.

What to expect

A taste unlike any other. I wish I could give you more. The Heart of Darkness is tart, sweet, and dark.

A drink after my own heart. No wonder I love it so!

. . .

Ingredients

(For activated charcoal raspberry preserves)

- 370g raspberry preserves
- Activated charcoal

(For cocktail)

- 1.5oz tequila
- 0.5oz Koch Espadin Mezcal
- 0.5oz lime juice
- 0.5oz agave syrup
- 1.5 teaspoons activated charcoal raspberry preserves
- Dash Xocolatl Mole bitters
- Ice cubes

Method

(For activated charcoal raspberry preserves)

1. Combine one 370g jar of raspberry preserves to 5 teaspoons of activated charcoal.
2. Blend to combine.

(For cocktail)

1. Combine ingredients except ice in a shaker.
2. Shake.
3. Pour over crushed ice.

OTHER BOOKS BY DANIEL WILLCOCKS

They Rot (Book 1 of 'The Rot' series)

They Remain (Book 2 of 'The Rot' series)

Lazarus: Enter the Deadspace

Twisted: A collection of dark shorts

Sins of Smoke

The Caitlin Chronicles

Dawn of Chaos (1)

Into The Fire (2)

Broken City (3)

Broken City (4)

Dan's Facebook Group

https://www.facebook.com/groups/832626480256677/

BOOKS BY MICHAEL ANDERLE

For a complete list of books by Michael Anderle, please visit:

www.lmbpn.com/ma-books/

CONNECT WITH THE AUTHORS

Dan Willcocks Social

Social media: @willcocksauthor
www.danielwillcocks.com
www.hawkandcleaver.com
https://www.acast.com/thestorystudio/tss028-20booksto50k-morew-michaelanderle

Michael Anderle Social

http://www.lmbpn.com
https://www.facebook.com/LMBPNPublishing
https://twitter.com/lmbpn
https://www.instagram.com/lmbpn_publishing/
https://www.bookbub.com/authors/michael-anderle